Three Little Kittens Learn a Lesson

by Bethany Lyons
Illustrated by Janet Skiles

PEARSON

Glenview, Illinois • Boston, Massachusetts • Chandler, Arizona
Upper Saddle River, New Jersey

MR. DO-RIGHT: Hello! I am Mr. Do-Right. Welcome to my T.V. talk show. This afternoon we are talking about being responsible.

The Three Little Kittens are here. You may know about them. There is a famous rhyme about them. Here is how it goes.

MR. DO-RIGHT *(singing the rhyme)*:
Three little kittens
They lost their mittens,
And they began to cry.
"Oh, Mother dear,
We sadly fear
Our mittens we have lost."

"What! Lost your mittens,
You naughty kittens!
Then you shall have no pie.
Meow, meow, meow.
You shall have no pie."

MR. DO-RIGHT: Let's talk to the three kittens! We will ask them what happened to their mittens.

MR. DO-RIGHT: How did you lose the mittens?

KITTEN ONE: We took them off when they got muddy. Then we played some more, and we forgot about our mittens.

KITTEN TWO: When we got home, we didn't have our mittens.

MR. DO-RIGHT: What did your mother say?

KITTEN THREE: She said we couldn't have pie. She said we should have taken better care of our mittens.

MR. DO-RIGHT: The rhyme also says, "The three little kittens, they found their mittens." Tell us about that.

KITTEN ONE: We wanted to solve our problem. We wanted to find the mittens. We went back to the playground. Our mittens were there, on the ground.

KITTEN TWO: Then we went home and washed our mittens. It was important to show Mother that we would try harder to take care of our things.

MR. DO-RIGHT: What did your mother do?

KITTEN THREE : She was pleased. She was happy with us. Then she gave us some pie.

MR. DO-RIGHT: What did you learn from this?

KITTEN ONE: We learned to take care of our things.

KITTEN TWO: To solve problems ourselves.

KITTEN THREE: To do the right thing!

MR. DO-RIGHT: Those are important things! Thank you, and good-bye, kittens!